VALERIE B.

grow with me

SNAKE

Published by Creative Paperbacks
P.O. Box 227, Mankato, Minnesota 56002
Creative Paperbacks is an imprint of
The Creative Company
www.thecreativecompany.us

Design by Ellen Huber
Production by Chelsey Luther
Art direction by Rita Marshall
Printed in the United States of America

Photographs by 123rf (Eric Chiang), Alamy (Picture
Press), Dreamstime (Amwu, Isselee), Getty Images
(Martin Harvey, Visuals Unlimited, Inc./Jim Merli),
iStockphoto (Brasil2, EcoPic), National Geographic
Stock (LUIS ESPIN, NORBERT ROSING, GORDON
WILTSIE), Shutterstock (Fribus Ekaterina, fivespots,
Eric Isselee, Heiko Kiera, mikeledray, noppharat, Dave
Welch), SuperStock (age fotostock, Animals Animals,
Biosphoto, John Cancalosi/age fotostock, Corbis,
imagebroker.net, Wayne Lynch/All Canada Photos,
NaturePL, NHPA, Robert Olenick/All Canada Photos)

Library of Congress Cataloging-in-Publication Data
Bodden, Valerie.
Snake / Valerie Bodden.
p. cm. — (Grow with me)
Includes bibliographical references and index.
Summary: An exploration of the life cycle and life
span of snakes, using up-close photographs and step-
by-step text to follow a snake's growth process from
egg to baby to mature snake.

ISBN 978-1-60818-406-4 (hardcover)
ISBN 978-0-89812-992-2 (pbk)
1. Snakes—Juvenile literature. 2. Snakes—Life cycles—
Juvenile literature. I. Title.
QL666.O6B684 2014
597.96—dc23   2013029626

CCSS: RI.3.1, 2, 3, 4, 5, 6, 7, 8; RI.4.1, 2, 3, 4, 5, 7; RF.3.3, 4

First Edition
9 8 7 6 5 4 3 2 1

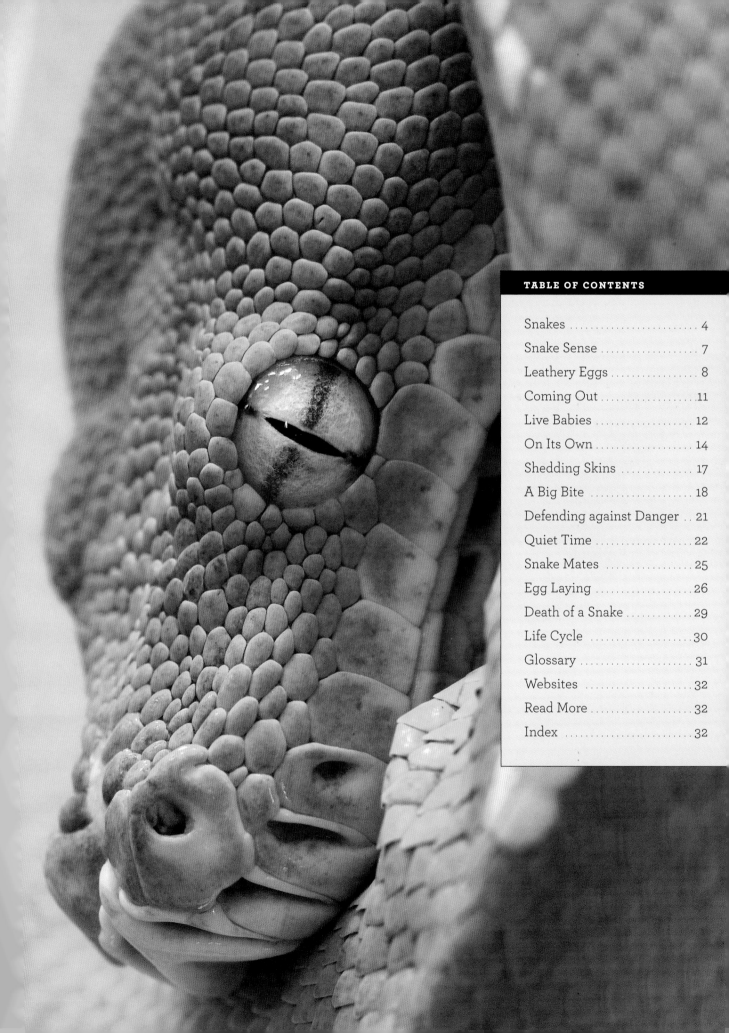

TABLE OF CONTENTS

Snakes are reptiles. Reptiles are **cold-blooded** animals covered with scales. Snakes have long, thin bodies with no legs.

Snakes live everywhere in the world except Antarctica and a few islands. They make their homes in deserts, wetlands, prairies, and **tropical rainforests**. Scientists have discovered about 2,900 **species** of snake.

Vipers live in the
Americas, Europe,
Asia, and Africa.

5

6

The dwarf puff
adder moves
sideways through
African sand.

The longest Cape cobra on record was 6.1 feet (1.9 m) long.

The smallest snake in the world is about the size of an earthworm. But the biggest snakes can be more than 30 feet (9.1 m) long and weigh more than 2 grown men! Some snakes are bright colors. Others are dull brown or gray to help them blend in with their surroundings.

Snakes cannot see or hear well. Instead, they feel **vibrations** in the ground. To smell, a snake "tastes" odors in the air with its forked tongue. It touches its tongue to the roof of its mouth. The odors pass through two holes called the Jacobson's **organ** there. Some snakes can sense body heat, too.

7

8

Most mother snakes lay between 3 and 16 eggs. They lay the eggs in a warm, moist, hidden spot. Sometimes eggs are laid in a cave or under rotting leaves.

A snake egg's shell is tough and leathery. It is usually white and oval-shaped. Small snake species usually lay smaller eggs than big snake species.

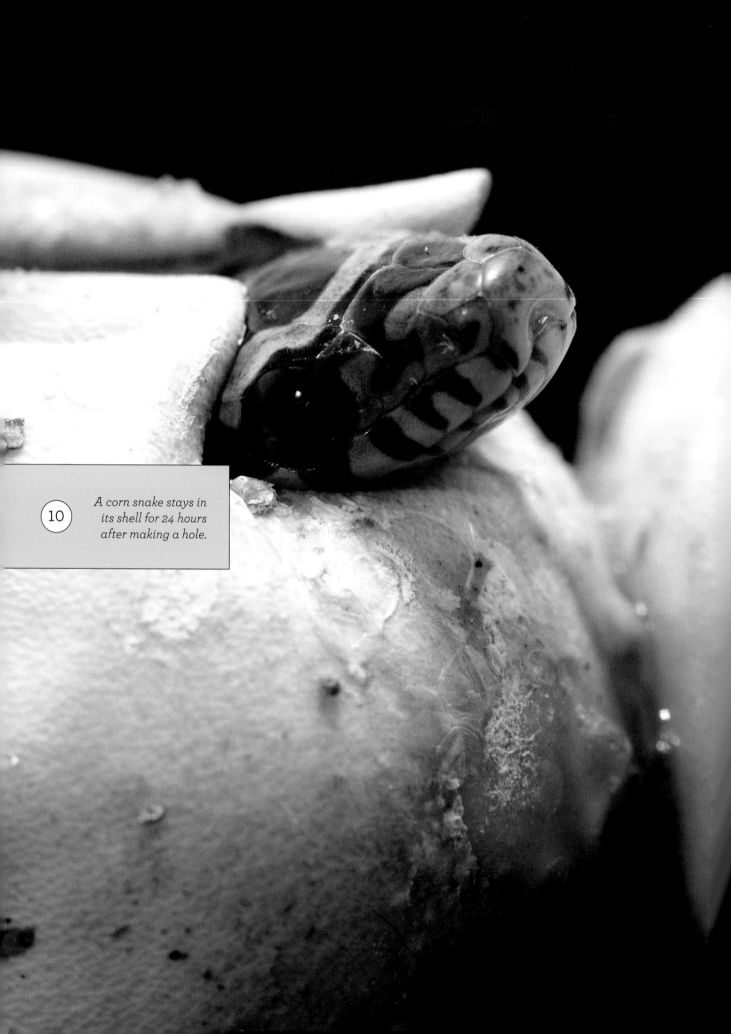

A corn snake stays in
its shell for 24 hours
after making a hole.

10

While it is inside the egg, a baby snake is called an **embryo** (*EM-bree-oh*). The embryo gets food from the **yolk** of the egg. Most baby snakes grow inside the egg for two or three months.

A baby snake breaks through its shell with its egg tooth. This small, sharp point on its nose falls off the first time the snake **molts**. The snake might rest in the shell a day or two before it wriggles away.

Some female snakes give birth to live young. The females carry their eggs inside their bodies. The eggs are covered with a **membrane** instead of a shell.

A mother snake can carry 5 to 50 eggs in her body at a time. The baby snakes are born after about three months. Live-born snakes have an egg tooth, too. They use it to get out of the membrane.

A mother diamond python cares for the eggs until they hatch.

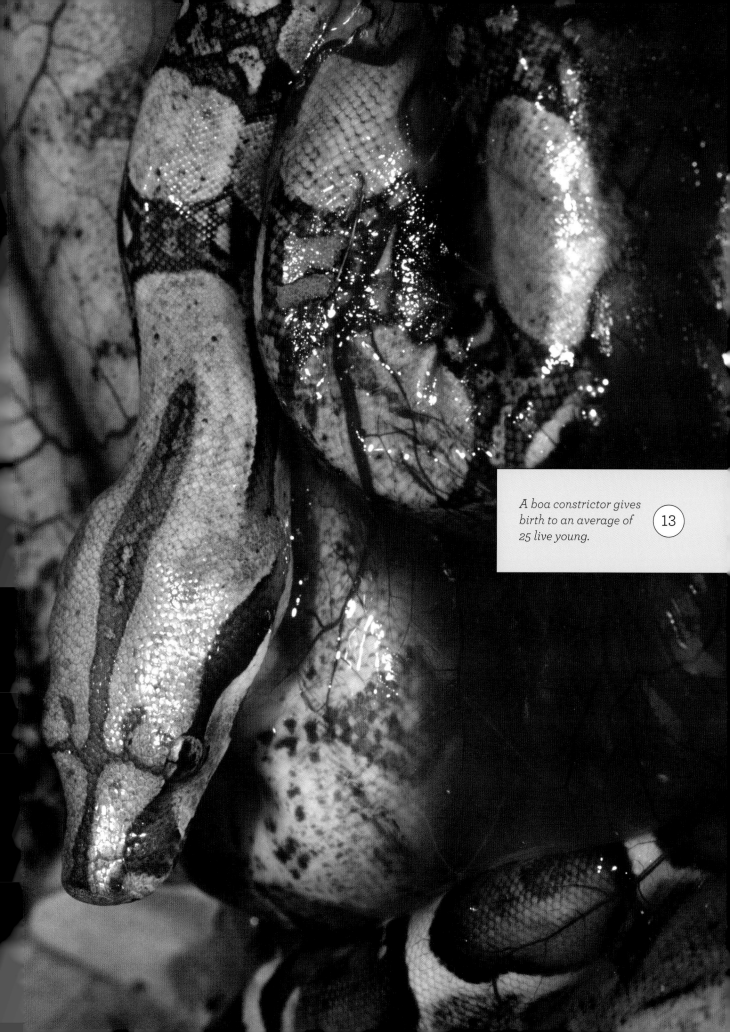

A boa constrictor gives birth to an average of 25 live young.

Mother snakes do not take care of their babies. But a baby snake is born knowing how to take care of itself.

It knows what kind of food to look for. Young snakes can capture small **prey** such as **insects**, frogs, and lizards. A baby snake knows how to protect itself, too. But many young snakes are still eaten by **predators** such as frogs, eagles, owls, and foxes.

14

Southern hognose snakes play dead to keep predators away.

Herons eat mainly fish and frogs but will catch snakes, too.

15

16 *Adult boa constrictors shed skin every two to four months.*

As the young snake grows, its skin gets too tight. About a week after it is born, the snake molts for the first time. A young snake can molt six or more times a year. Older snakes might molt only two or three times a year.

A snake loosens its old skin by rubbing its head against a rock or a tree. The skin breaks open, and the snake slides out of it. A young snake's skin can change colors as the snake gets older.

17

Snake scales are smooth (pictured) or keeled, with a ridge in the center.

Most snakes hide and wait for prey. Then they grab the animal. Some snakes bite their prey with **fangs**. The fangs of some snakes send **venom** into the prey. Other snakes constrict, or squeeze, their prey until it dies.

Snakes eat mice, lizards, birds, eggs, and fish. Big snakes can eat pigs, raccoons, and even deer. Snakes swallow their prey whole. Some snakes can go more than a month be-tween meals!

18

Like all vipers, sedge vipers are venomous snakes with fangs.

Tropical snakes such as sipos look for tree frogs to eat.

Prairie rattlesnakes raise their bodies and shake their tails in warning.

20

A growing snake faces many dangers. Eagles, crocodiles, and raccoons all eat snakes. People kill snakes for their skin or to make medicine.

When a snake is threatened, it might bite. But first it usually gives a warning. It might hiss or squirt a smelly liquid. Rattlesnakes shake the rattle on their tail. Some snakes are brightly colored to let others know that their bite is **poisonous**.

21

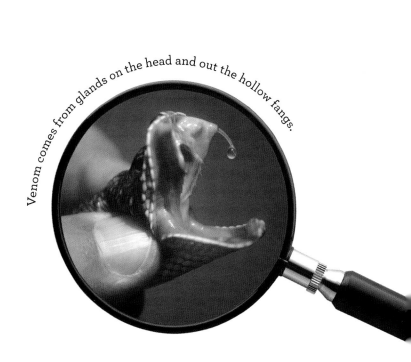

Venom comes from glands on the head and out the hollow fangs.

Springtime brings garter snakes out of hibernation.

A snake is cold-blooded, so it has to keep its body the right temperature. If it gets too cold, it cannot move around or digest its food. A snake lies in the sun to warm up. When it gets too hot, it moves into the shade or underground.

Snakes that live in cool climates **hibernate** during the winter. Hundreds of snakes can hibernate together in underground dens or caves. Some desert snakes stay underground and do not move around during the hottest times of year.

22

Green tree pythons (often yellow when young) dangle their tail to attract prey.

23

24 Male garter snakes surround a female in a "mating ball."

Most snakes become fully grown between the ages of two and five. Then they look for a mate. Female snakes give off special scents, called pheromones, when they are ready to mate.

Sometimes two males fight over a female. They might wrap their bodies around each other. The strongest snake gets to mate with the female. Some males mate with more than one female.

25

Two Panamint rattlesnake males try to outdo each other in a combat dance.

Snakes live alone unless they are looking for a mate.

26

After they mate, males and females do not stay together. The female snake looks for a safe place to lay her eggs. She might use the same spot every year. The female lays her eggs two to four months after mating.

Females of most snake species leave their eggs. But a few guard them from predators. Pythons even wrap their bodies around the eggs to keep them warm. Snakes that do not lay eggs usually have their babies a couple months after mating.

Taiwan beauty rat snakes coil around their eggs from a few hours up to 60 days.

27

28 *Python hatchlings are generally 18 to 24 inches (46–61 cm) long.*

DEATH OF A SNAKE

Snakes can live about 20 years in the wild. Most snakes mate every year. And every year, females lay more eggs. Each of those eggs can become a new snake. That snake will have scaly babies of its own.

29

Snakes that are kept in zoos or as pets can live up to 40 years.

A snake lays 3 to 16 eggs in a warm hiding place.

Snake eggs hatch in  2 to 3 months.

The snake rests in the egg for 1 or 2 days.

The snake molts for the first time when it is about 1 week old.

The snake molts 6 or more times a year for its first few years.

Between the ages of 2 and 5,  a snake mates.

Two to 4 months after mating, the female lays her eggs.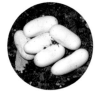

The snake continues to mate and molt for the rest of its life.

 Around age 20, the snake dies.

cold-blooded: *having a body temperature that is affected by the surrounding air temperature*

embryo: *an offspring that has not hatched out of an egg yet*

fangs: *long, sharp teeth*

hibernate: *to spend the winter sleeping or not moving around much*

insects: *animals that have six legs and one or two pairs of wings*

membrane: *a thin layer that covers or separates parts of an animal*

molts: *loses an old skin and grows a new one*

organ: *a part of an animal's body that does a certain job*

poisonous: *causing death or illness*

predators: *animals that kill and eat other animals*

prey: *animals that are killed and eaten by other animals*

species: *groups of living things that are closely related*

tropical rainforests: *hot and wet places where many plants grow; they are found in the hottest parts of the world*

venom: *a poison made by an animal such as a snake*

vibrations: *back-and-forth movements*

yolk: *the middle, yellow part of an egg that contains food for a growing embryo*

31

WEBSITES

Kidzone: Snakes

http://www.kidzone.ws/lw/snakes/index.htm

Check out snake activities, facts, and pictures.

National Geographic Kids: Rattlesnakes

http://kids.nationalgeographic.com/kids/animals/creaturefeature/rattlesnakes/

Find facts, pictures, and videos of snakes.

Note: Every effort has been made to ensure that the websites listed above are suitable for children, that they have educational value, and that they contain no inappropriate material. However, because of the nature of the Internet, it is impossible to guarantee that these sites will remain active indefinitely or that their contents will not be altered.

READ MORE

Bodden, Valerie. *Snakes*.
Mankato, Minn.: Creative Education, 2010.

Hoff, Mary. *Snakes*.
Mankato, Minn.: Creative Education, 2007.

INDEX